The Road To $20 Million

Bankruptcy to Multi-Million Dollar Real Estate Producer

Shane Torres

D1529183

ISBN-13: 978-0-578-49781-5

For information about special discounts for bulk purchases, please contact Shane Torres, shane@roadto20million.com or visit www.roadto20million.com.

GRAB YOUR FREE GIFT!

READ THIS FIRST

Just to say thanks for buying my book, I would like to give you my mindset and goal setting roadmap 100% FREE!

TO DOWNLOAD GO TO:
http://roadto20million.com/RT2Mbookgift

Dedication and Thank You

To my wife Mandy and children, Andi, Cohan.

And Gavin; thank you for always supporting me in everything I do.

Table of Contents

PART ONE: THE BREAKDOWN 1

    Chapter One: The Fall 3

    Chapter Two: My Lowest Point 9

PART TWO: HEADED IN THE RIGHT DIRECTION .. 13

    Chapter Three: Running On Fumes.......................... 15

    Chapter Four: Sitting Courtside 19

    Chapter Five: Reading the Road Signs...................... 25

    Chapter Six: Opportunity is Now Here...................... 29

PART THREE: THE ROADMAP 53

    Chapter Seven: Determine Your Destination................ 55

    Chapter Eight: Plan For Passengers 59

    Chapter Nine: Find Your Fuel & Efficiency.................. 63

    Chapter Ten: Engage In The Journey........................ 69

    Chapter Eleven: Explore Your Options (for Business
    Entrepreneurs).. 73

    Chapter Twelve: Drive Your Brand and Your Business...... 75

    Chapter Thirteen: Enjoy The Ride and See The Sights 81

NEXT STEPS.. 85

ABOUT THE AUTHOR 87

Note from the Author

The Road to $20 Million was created to redefine the journey to success and make it attainable for everyone; using my own path to success.

From the things that worked well and the lessons I learned along the way.

It's my hope that you'll avoid the pitfalls and mistakes I made, and fast-track your own success through what you learn in this book.

Shane Torres

PART ONE:
THE BREAKDOWN

CHAPTER ONE:

The Fall

Tuesday, March 2009. As I sat in my truck, at a jobsite on the NW side of Des Moines, my 3rd that morning, it hit me.

At this point in my life, and where I was with my construction business, there were nights where I didn't sleep. Most days I didn't eat and when I did eat, I got sick. The stress of the company was affecting my family, my health, my marriage and my life.

I was on the phone with my wife, Mandy, and the realization struck like a 2x4 to the head. Through a fog of uncertainty and frustration, I said the words, "I can't do it anymore."

"What do you mean you can't do it anymore?"

At that point I broke down.

We had ten or twelve projects going on, a multi-million dollar construction business, and I realized that I wasn't going to be able to proceed with any of it.

Just uttering the words, admitting to myself and my wife that I'd had it, it was like a big weight was lifted off my shoulders, even though I knew it wasn't over… in fact, it was just beginning.

At the end of the day on Thursday of that same week, I grabbed my laptop, set my keys to the company truck and office on the counter, walked out, and took my personal truck home.

I was done.

At four o'clock in the morning on Friday (the next day) I sent an email. I had told myself I was going to be able to sit down with each person individually and tell them what was happening but when the time came, I didn't have the courage to do so. I was too weak.

So, I emailed everyone with tears pouring down my face, barely able to type, and let them know that we were shutting the company down and it was over.

By eight o'clock my phone was blowing up with people trying to talk to me — contractors, clients, banks, partners. Some were wanting answers, others were just furious.

I was actually sitting in the parking lot of Consumer Credit of Des Moines waiting for the office to open while people were trying to get a hold of me — all the while knowing I was going to have to file for bankruptcy. As I sent every call to voicemail, each one stinging for different reasons, I sat there in tears and again reflected on how I got here.

At the time, I had just turned 30. My 5 year old company had grown from a few projects in the early days to large retirement centers and hotels. We had 40 full-time employees at the peak with an additional 100+ sub-contractors.

To keep our growth curve moving in the right direction, we did a little of everything: we built new homes, had framing and siding crews, we did remodeling, some light commercial general contracting. In the winter we did snow removal with the 10 trucks that had snow plows and a couple of skid loaders.

For 4-5 years I had everything under control (or so I thought). Looking back, I was 10 feet tall and bulletproof.

We weren't looking at the downside risk of our decisions.

We were ordering custom trucks and spending money we shouldn't have spent on other "necessities."

In addition, several of the bigger jobs were problematic as the materials that were ordered didn't match our plans. I was facing having to absorb tens of thousands in losses on ordering and processing errors. We weren't saving money as a company and eventually I found myself sacrificing my own personal finances to help fund the business.

My pride was tied up in the success of the business and my pristine credit score that I had worked so hard to rebuild.

So money was spent on equipment and property leases that realistically should have been renegotiated. Our overhead was bloated, but my ego got in the way of handling that in the moment. I just assumed there would always be more work, and as a result, I'd always be driving forward.

Unfortunately, that was not the case.

As for that day, I had to see what bankruptcy looked like. I had no money at that point, so even to file the Chapter 7, I had to borrow the money from my aunt.

I did end up talking to a few people that called that day, ultimately learning who friends were and who they weren't. By the time I was done, I really didn't have anyone left that I saw as friends.

The lawsuits and threats started almost immediately — even threats to my children and wife.

CHAPTER TWO:

My Lowest Point

For the past decade I had lived my life by the motto: Without work, there's nothing else.

All of my pride, ego and self-worth had been tied to the business, and now, it felt like I had nothing. No pressing business to attend to, no one calling for guidance or direction, no big decisions to be made. I felt lost and was in a very dark place.

I was still going through the motions, getting up early, getting online to look for jobs, but I wanted nothing to do with construction, or with home building. I was applying for jobs in Kansas City, Chicago, and Minneapolis and getting rejected left and right. I was told they were not hiring due to downturn or I was overqualified.

Over the next 30-60 days, I literally just shut down and locked myself in the basement — phone off, watching

TV. Lost in 90's TV shows like "Las Vegas" and "90210." It was my escape from reality and my previous world that was burning around me.

I felt like I had let everyone down and was a failure as a provider for my family.

Each conversation or trip out of the house was a reminder of how I failed myself and everyone around me. I couldn't talk to anyone about it without breaking down.

During that time, I ballooned to my highest weight ever — 260 pounds. My sleep was irregular, my food intake was terrible, and I was living on a steady diet of *Zantac* and *Aleve*.

In the midst of television watching, some word or phrase would trigger a memory and I'd relive some aspect of what had happened and what I could've done differently to alter my circumstances. I would just sit there and think about what I could have done differently over and over again.

In one of my absolute low points, Mandy and I had a pivotal conversation that turned things around. In the midst of an emotional breakdown, I reminded Mandy that in my 20's I wanted to be worth a million dollars by the time I hit 40. But by the age of 30, I'd hit that mark and lost it all.

I remember asking her, "If you obtain a goal and then you lose it, does it count? Did you still obtain that goal?" It was almost as if the success I'd had was no longer on my scorecard. I had what I thought was the most important thing, and now the thought of not having it was keeping me depressed.

"What did you lose that mattered?" She asked me back.

That night I didn't sleep. I thought about what she'd said. I lost money. I lost cars. I lost houses. I lost what I thought were friends.

My family was still there. My kids were still there. I was way overweight but semi-healthy. What really mattered I still had, but I'd have to change the road I was on if things were going to get better.

The next day I made a conscious decision that I was going to change direction. I sold my Bowflex, which sat unused in the corner of the basement covered in clothes, and bought a one year membership to a gym. After 10 years of "not having time to work out," I now had nothing but time to exercise and start working on myself.

As a former high school athlete who was fairly strong and fast, the first several weeks at the gym were humbling. I could barely walk on a treadmill or lift anything without having to stop to catch my breath.

Within 90 days, working out 4-6 times a week, I had dropped 30 pounds and was close to lifting the same amount I could in my early 20's. (To this day, I work out 3-6 days a week and attribute my energy level and mental focus to that habit and having a routine.)

Looking back at that one simple question, *"what did you lose that mattered?,"* that conversation with Mandy was the turning point.

PART TWO:
HEADED IN THE RIGHT
DIRECTION

CHAPTER THREE:

Running On Fumes

My next step was figuring out what I was going to do for work. The daily exercise was good for me, if nothing else than to give me somewhere to go and a sense of purpose, but I was needing both something to attach myself to and a way of providing for my family.

Fortunately, my accountant had me paying myself as a W2 employee of my own company which made me eligible for unemployment benefits. The $300 a week we were receiving essentially covered necessities and allowed us to pay whatever bill was going to get shut off next.

We were blessed with extensions to this a few times due to things the state government allowed. Without those extensions, I don't know what would've happened.

Our mortgage wasn't getting paid and every month we lurked closer and closer to foreclosure. Growing up we received food assistance and I had vowed that I would never have to do that, so it was a very low point for me when I had to file for food assistance to feed my family.

Before the business tumbled, I used to have a limited mindset as it related to giving. If we didn't have the money, we generally wouldn't give very much. Our new situation was a wake up call in more ways than one however, and my wife and I agreed that we had to start giving first and put our faith in God that He would provide.

We relied on family heavily during this period. My aunt and uncle had offered me the opportunity to drive trucks for their directional drilling company. They knew we were in a challenging spot and the offer was a lifeline for our finances. So they paid for me to get my Commercial Driver's License (CDL) and started making plans for me to be a part of their team. The job itself was an over-the-road truck driving job that would have me away from home up to 8 or 9 months a year. It wasn't ideal, but it wasn't working in construction either.

To add another wrinkle in our plan, just before I was to start the job, we found out that Mandy was expecting our third child. So on top of the financial mess our lives were in, at the beginning of foreclosure—not sure of the road I was supposed to be taking, God blessed us with another mouth to feed.

Finding out we were going to have a our third child, I believe, came at the perfect time. During a late night conversation, Mandy admitted that she didn't want me on the road working away from home. Although she had no desire to move from our house, she would rather lose the house than have me on the road all of the time.

By the next morning I had made up my mind — I was going to turn down the truck driving job and I would do everything in my power to keep the house. While I wasn't positive that we could avoid foreclosure, I decided that I was going to do my absolute best to save it. I was prepared for the consequences if I didn't, but I had to be able to say I'd tried my best.

Since I had decided not to become a truck driver, I had to figure out what my options were.

At the end of 2008, I had started taking classes to get my real estate license. I had completed the course and taken the test, but only passed the national test the first time and had failed the state test twice. Having been in the construction industry, I assumed the test would be a breeze. Testing was not a strength of mine however, and since I hadn't passed the state test, I had let that option go while I was going through the loss of my company and battling depression. I had no money to take the test again, so I borrowed from my father-in-law, bought a study guide at the Des Moines Association of Realtors office, and committed to passing on my third attempt.

An hour ahead of my test, I sat in the parking lot and went through that study guide back and forth, back and forth. When it was time, I immediately went in, took the test, and passed it.

My journey as a real estate agent could now begin.

CHAPTER FOUR:

Sitting Courtside

When my business finally collapsed, there were a number of companies who were (understandably) upset. So for the next 18 months, while I was starting my journey in real estate, I also spent a good portion of my time dealing with lawsuits.

While most of the suits got dismissed in the bankruptcy, one of the larger banks in town decided to dispute the bankruptcy and sue me for upwards of $400,000.

After reviewing the quotes from attorneys to defend me, most in the $20-30,000 range, I responded to the suit and decided to defend myself in court (I was fortunate that an attorney friend was giving me free advice).

I'm not sure if it was me being naive or just a feeling like I had nothing else to lose by doing it, that prompted me to make that choice. But because I couldn't afford to pay an attorney, I went after the trial just like I was going after saving my house from foreclosure, getting healthy, and building the real estate business.

I was going to do my best.

Most people involved in the trial were surprised at my decision. Those on the other side of the courtroom tried to play that against me — the fact that I didn't really know what I was doing. They tried to get things dismissed right away because I didn't answer questions in the proper fashion. I was fortunate in the fact that the judge saw that I was at least trying and didn't hold my ignorance of the process against me. She did not allow them to dismiss anything.

It was at that moment I knew I could win.

I found the biggest challenge was everyday questioning what to do and how to do it. When you get a response from an attorney, you literally have to go through the whole document line item by line item and address each individual one. Keep in mind, I didn't go to school for this. I'm not the best writer or speller, my grammar isn't perfect. It was a tedious process and my family's financial future was riding somewhat on the outcome of the case.

The court case was an 18-month process, in and out of federal court.

During one court date the attorney called me to the stand and questioned me, then called the bank's lender to the stand and questioned him. When it came time for me to cross-examine the lender, I basically used similar questions and came up with material on the fly.

Going into a federal courthouse, you're not allowed to take your cellphone so you're literally going in on your own and it's a scary feeling.

When the final day in court came, closing arguments were given and I learned (the hard way) you cannot object in a final closing statement. The judge does not like that. Nevertheless, my year and a half of defending myself came to an end. It took 60 days to get the judges verdict — about 95% of the case was dismissed.

I ended up owing the bank less than 10% of the original amount of the case.

We're from the IRS and we're here to help

If you've ever heard that the IRS won't call you or send you a text message, that's true. What they will do is make house calls. They'll do it more than once, if need be. And if they do, it's time to take them very seriously.

To add insult to injury, when things got tight with the construction company, we had fallen behind on our payroll taxes. We had about $100,000 in IRS debt and I found out there's two things you can't get rid of in a bankruptcy: payroll taxes and student loans.

Again, I was very fortunate with the IRS agent I was given because she helped me navigate through that situation.

One thing I realized was that even when you owe people or organizations money, they're very willing to help you sort things out if you're upfront about your willingness to pay, but also your inability to pay the whole amount. In the end, the $100,000 I originally owed was successfully negotiated down to about $48,000.

The IRS agent then helped me put the debt in a deferment status because I had no money at the time to cover the payments. Deferment essentially meant they were going to charge interest and let it add up but they weren't going to try to collect until things got sorted out.

About the middle of 2012, I called them and said, "Hey, I'm ready to work out a payment plan."

All along I had the mindset that I was going to do my absolute best to make everything right in all scenarios. Knowing at that point that my family needed me to succeed. If I failed, at least I could say I tried.

That is how I got by, and how I still approach things to this day.

CHAPTER FIVE:

Reading the Road Signs

It's often said that the closer you are to rock bottom, the more clearly you're able to see things.

One day I took my kids up to the town square to play at the park (in the midst of these big life altering decisions I was making). Mandy was off at an appointment and I happened to be at home with the kids. While watching them play on the equipment, it suddenly occurred to me that this was the first time I'd ever taken them to the park. My kids were five and three at the time and I was experiencing the joy of being at the park with them for the first time as a parent.

Money and business and "having stuff" was more important to me before than carving out time for my kids.

These "road signs" started showing up everywhere highlighting something I was supposed to see, a path to follow, perhaps a lesson to learn. Being with my kids told me I should live more in line with my values, which prompted me to actually write down what I valued.

I started with family. The park was a sign that whatever I was going to pursue had to have family as a priority. I made a decision right then that If I was in town, I was going to be at every single event they had. Balance and the appropriate use of my time, relative to me valuing my family, was critical.

The money challenges we were having was a sign that I had been working hard for money, but for all the wrong reasons. It wasn't to help other people so much as it was to satisfy my ego or prove my naysayers wrong. It occurred to me that if I was taking care of other people, the money would ultimately take care of itself. While it wasn't immediately clear, I was going through this mess so that *I could help* other people through theirs.

To this day helping someone with a short sale, avoid foreclosure or helping one of our agents with something personal, is an incredible feeling.

The finances (and three kids and a wife) kept me hungry for success during this time.

What I can only call "opportunities" kept popping up at just the right time. We chalked it up to God's provisions, but everytime it felt like we were on our last nickel, something would drop in our laps that provided.

There were times that I had my doubts, when it was particularly rough, and we were running out of money. At one point I said to Mandy, "I know God's got a plan but I need a sign I'm making the right decision here." The next day I got a check in the mail for just over $7,000. That was the sign I had asked for, and God had provided.

In fact, it reminded me of the story of the man stuck on the roof of a home surrounded by rising flood waters.

After praying for God to save him, a neighbor came by in a canoe offering him a ride to safety. "No thanks, God is going to save me."

More prayers to God and along comes a rescue worker in a speedboat offering a ride to safety. "No thanks, God is going to save me."

The water continues to rise and after more desperate prayer, a helicopter flies overhead dropping a rescue line. "No thanks, God is going to save me."

The man eventually dies in the flood waters and arrives at the pearly gates. "Lord, why didn't you save me from the floodwaters?"

God responds, "I sent your neighbor, a rescue worker, and a helicopter. Were you looking for a miracle?"

Another sign that our tithes and prayers were working were the continued opportunities that came up when we needed them most. Whether it was an unexpected tax refund, a request from a friend to help with some construction projects, or a job offer pushing snow in the winter, I was reading the signs and following the opportunities.

While some people read 'Opportunity is Nowhere', I was reading 'Opportunity is Now Here'.

Those opportunities became the cornerstone of building a $20M+ real estate company.

CHAPTER SIX:

Opportunity is Now Here

They tell you when you get into real estate that you need to have a sphere. You need to have a network of people and you need to have groups you're a part of to get referrals from. I didn't have any of that. In fact, most of the people in my life had turned their backs on me. I was having to start from scratch.

At this point, I had declared bankruptcy, was facing foreclosure, battling a bank in court, negotiating with the IRS and had a wife and three little ones at home. To top it off, I was starting a business that the experts say takes at least three years to achieve "stability."

And yet, I saw opportunity.

Larger numbers of foreclosures were happening in 2009 and early 2010, and with my experience personally, I thought 'why not start here?'

Days on end I spent contacting foreclosure agents but none of them were replying. So, I contacted my broker at the time and asked, "Hey, how do I get in on these? Because I think I can do a pretty good job here."

When I started going through the list of asset management companies, I realized it's extremely hard to get into foreclosures, mostly due to the fact there were so many people doing it. You basically had to know someone in the banks or asset companies to get started but by signing up for REO (Foreclosures), you also get signed up for a BPO which is a Broker Price Opinion.

Essentially, a BPO is ordered by the bank to get an idea of the value of the home in foreclosure. Agents are hired to go out to do an assessment of the value of a home. Once an agent agrees to the BPO, finishes the report and turns it in, the companies will pay the agent $50 on average per BPO Report. Now, $50 may not seem like much, but I was willing to do whatever it took to build my business, keep my family afloat, and stay in my home.

On the very first BPO, I was asked if I'd go to a town an hour and a half away in the middle of a sleet storm.

While I wanted to say no, I said "yes" to build that relationship.

You are also graded as a provider of BPOs. The more I did, the higher my grade went. I must have crossed a major threshold of service, because I got a phone call asking me how many I could handle. The servicer had just taken on one of the largest lenders in the nation and had BPO orders to fill on a daily basis. The opportunity was now here and I told them, "as many as you can send me."

I would go on to become the largest BPO Agent in the state.

Three things happened as a result of me taking on this opportunity:

First, the income that came in from doing BPOs was extremely helpful in getting our family through some lean times. That second year (2010) in real estate, I did over 1,000 BPOs and made over $50,000 from the servicer. Easily more than anyone else in the Midwest was doing on their own.

Second, and as a by-product of having to complete 1,000 BPOs, I focused on building really effective systems that allowed me to get them done quickly, without taking too much time away from other business building activities. That mentality around systems has been a cornerstone of how I've built my business over time. The systems run the business and the people run the systems.

Third, because I was visiting so many foreclosures and looking at so many valuations, I knew my market like the back of my hand. There's really only one way to get to know your market and that is to actually be out there seeing it! With 1,000 of these visits under my belt, I was absolutely confident, at listing appointments, about the price points for various homes. In fact, it was almost second nature.

I didn't do anything as far as setting the world on fire in sales. My very first year (2009) I only sold three homes and made around $13,000 so it wasn't much. But in 2010, my second year in the business, I cleared over $100,000 between BPO revenue and sales commissions.

When I tell people that I did that many BPO's, they're shocked.

To be honest, I was running ragged. I was running from this one to the next and I wasn't very smart with my time. Then I got to a point where I got smart about how I scheduled my day.

I would get up early in the morning. I would do my marketing and emails. I would do data input with BPO's and then would go out in the afternoon and take photos of the BPO's I needed to do for the day. It was structured in such a way that I was able to fill it in with any appointments that I had. I literally scheduled everything into a big circle.

A system was finally put in place where I was able to sit down with all of my data and photos, and I could pump out one BPO in fifteen minutes. It was definitely hustling.

It got to a point where I was doing so many BPO's I would send Mandy out to take photos of the properties for me and then I would do the data input the next morning. I had to do that otherwise I was gone more than I wanted to be and I still struggled with that a little bit in the beginning. Not a little bit... I struggled with it a lot just like most do.

The busier I got in real estate, the more I cut back on BPOs because I just didn't have time to do them. So, in 2010, I did 1,000 and then I did 600 the next year and then it just started to trickle down to doing none.

On any given morning, I might get a few orders, even to this day. I've tried in the past to help people get into them because it is a good supplemental income, but they just don't understand the opportunity and give up.

Around the same time I started applying for all those BPO companies, I took my first short sale class. At the time, I didn't have any money and the National Association was bringing a series of classes to the Des Moines area that would result in a designation. In truth, I didn't know what I was signing up for. I knew it was normally $250 a class and they had it on sale for $75. I thought, "I can afford this and they say you need designations, so why not?" So, I started by signing up for two classes.

As I was sitting through the first class, presented by LeRoy Houser, a well-known coach, listening to him going through all of the short sale information, I thought, "this is genius." This is what I've got to focus on. I took that packet and knew I needed to know more.

The next class I went to featured a speaker from Chicago, so I got his whole perspective on the distressed market from his territory. At this point, I was starting to take the packets from both classes and create my own. I hadn't really started marketing yet, I'd just started to dabble in it, so I was getting a few short sales just by chance.

In the Fall of 2010, our company brought another company to town to certify agents as CDPE which is Certified Distressed Property Expert. This particular instructor was from Minneapolis, so again I got another perspective of another market. After that class was done, I gathered all three materials from each class, took what I liked from all three of them, and created my own pre-listing short sale packet.

By late Fall, I had marketing postcards created, and started to send the postcards to distressed properties. A few months later, the floodgates opened because of the system that I had created. Because I was going through foreclosure myself at the time, I could relate to what the people were going through.

At one point, I was managing 50-60 short sales at a time, processing them by myself, doing the follow-up by myself on a weekly basis. I controlled 25% of the short sale market in the area. To this day, I still have over 95% success rate in completion of those short sales.

My go-to for finding pre-foreclosures was RealtyTrac (https://www.realtytrac.com/), a foreclosure search website. I still, to this day, have a subscription to RealtyTrac and I send postcards to the list on that site every month. It's all about power in numbers. When you're sending out a couple hundred postcards a month, you only need one or two to make it worthwhile.

What started to happen was, these pre-foreclosure situations were in isolated areas in neighborhoods. Even though I didn't live there, I started becoming the go-to agent in those neighborhoods.

When I saw some business coming from a particular area, I'd throw up a bus bench ad in those neighborhoods with a very powerful message which then lead to me getting bigger short sales. They started off as smaller ones, but eventually I was doing $500,000-$1,000,000 short sales.

What most people didn't understand at the time was that what was happening in the housing market didn't just affect the middle class or the low-income families. It affected all families, including millionaires who had lost everything, some you would have never imagined being impacted. So, it was not uncommon to see million-dollar homes being foreclosed on and happening in short sales.

The South Side of the Des Moines metro took a huge hit. Because of the distressed property marketing I had in that area, I started getting an abundance of short sales. At one point I had 20 or 30 signs up in that community and decided to install a bus bench ad (which is still there to this day). As a result, people started to think I was from the Southside.

At the time, a lot of people were saying, "Oh, I don't wanna do that. It's too far from home" or "I don't wanna get up that early to do the work necessary to sell those."

What I saw was these people needed help. So, if they were engaged and willing to work and cooperate with me, I was gonna help them. It didn't matter to me what I was going to make from them. At the end of the day, it all added up.

It all started with that first class that I went to, and seeing the genius in the short sale process. They literally said, *the government is putting this law into effect that would forgive sellers tax liabilities. Banks will tell you exactly what they will sell these homes for. As long as you understand who you're dealing with, they're giving you the price.*

Then they started incentivizing clients to do short sales. Giving them checks for anywhere from a $1,000 to $20,000 dollars. If you're in foreclosure and someone's offering you $20,000, you're going to cooperate.

Opening my first office

We've lived in Polk City, Iowa for over a decade and by 2012 I'd started to crawl out of a hole, I was making a little bit of money, and I kept driving by an open office space to check my mail. I drove by that office space twice a day. Finally, I looked at it and the rent was really cheap. I just kept looking at it and going back to it. This went on for a few months.

In early 2012, I called the owner of our real estate company and asked, "Hey, has this ever been done?" and he said, "No, but I don't see why we can't." He owned the rights to everything at the time and I needed permission to open that office and use the RE/MAX name. I was an independent agent (as normal), but paid for all of the overhead in that office. I opened my first office in the Spring of 2012.

At the time, I had been working with a virtual assistant who did much of the detail oriented work. When the office opened, I brought her in-house. She answered phones. She was my office manager. She worked with our transaction coordinator. She was marketing. She helped put systems into place. If I had a new idea, she would help create it and make it look good. She did basically everything.

Because the traditional business was starting to grow, in 2012 I started to invest in marketing a little bit more in my local community. I became more involved by being seen at local events and by joining the Polk City Chamber of Commerce. A chamber of commerce (or board of trade) is an organization of businesses whose goal is to further the interests of the businesses and is also a great networking opportunity. That slowly took off and after 18 months, we just kind of blew up in the local area too. We were a prominent player in two markets which then snowballed into other markets.

Getting involved in the chamber organization is an incredible, yet affordable, way to get your name out in the community. To join the chamber as a member it was only $165 (every chamber is different). After the first few months, someone nominated me to be on the board. My response was, "Okay, fine. I don't know what that means but yeah, sure."

As our kids were getting older and involved in more activities, I was starting to be seen more and more in the community. I had been on the board for a year or so and at the time the local chamber was kind of in disarray. Just bad vibes given off by a lot of people.

After a few years on the board, I was asked to be chamber president. That gave me a whole different level of exposure because the next thing you know I'm doing ribbon cuttings, I'm giving speeches, I'm in the papers.

The folks in town began to tie that together with my signs and my mailers.

With the local chamber membership, I also became a member of the Greater Des Moines Partnership, the official economic group of Des Moines and its surrounding communities. This was when I started to realize the magic was in the partnership with the chamber. For a very nominal fee, you get to rub elbows with some of the most powerful people in Central Iowa, which normally you wouldn't even get close to in any other circumstance. So, I started going to more of those networking opportunities.

When I took over as chamber president, I think we had 19 members locally. Within a year we were back up to 40 members and the chamber was breaking even and not losing money. It's not a profit center but you never want to lose money! The next year, no one wanted to step up and be chamber president and while it's only supposed to be one term, I volunteered for a second term. As chamber president, you take a trip to Washington D.C. and, again, you have literally 200 of the most powerful people in Central Iowa in one location. It was great exposure, and an opportunity I was afforded both years.

After my second year, my term as chamber president was up, but I got a message from one of the directors at the Partnership asking for a meeting. Not knowing what I was walking into, when I got there they asked me if I would consider being a chair of the Affiliates Council. Essentially, asking me to be the head of all presidents of all the chambers in the region. And my response was, "Why not?"

The level of exposure was huge because it put me at the head table. It put me on the Partnership Executive Board which is year after year named the most influential board in Central Iowa. I used to joke that it was 19 important people and me.

When I went to the D.C. trip that year, I had to speak in front of those 200 people I was with as chamber president the 2 years before. Now, I'm a small town Iowa kid and I was sitting at dinner with the head general of Iowa military and congressmen and senators and CEOs — all for $165 bucks a year.

To this day it has been the best investment in my business, by far.

The entire time, I was also farming in specific markets. Most people think about farming as just applying to mailers, but it's not. It's being seen in any form or fashion you can. I was still doing the mailers, but I was starting to dabble a little bit in other areas as well. I started sponsoring some baseball teams and getting a little bit more involved in sponsoring the booster club and the high school.

After about 18 months, whether it was on the listing side or the buying side, our group was (and still is) involved in over 90% of the transactions in this smaller town.

In early 2013 I started to think, "You know, this is not that hard." I don't understand why other people aren't getting involved, why they're not farming their own community.

To this day, I preach these things and people still don't do it. Most people sign up for the chamber as an example and they think, "Oh, I didn't get anything on my return."

So I ask:

"Well, how many events did you go to?"

"Well, none."

"How many committees are you on?"

"Well, none."

"Well, what did you expect to get?"

One gentleman, who owned a local bar, got frustrated once and said, "I don't wanna do it anymore. I spend money doing this and doing that and over at that school —do you think they come over here? Do you think they come into my establishment after those games?" and I said, "When was the last time you went to a basketball game?"

"What do you mean?"

"When was the last time you went to any event?"

"Well, I haven't."

"Well, they don't know you. Why do you expect them to come into your establishment?"

Just because you give money to something doesn't mean they're gonna show up. They don't know you.

Hiring Employees Again

The scariest thing I ever did after losing what I did in 2009, was bringing on that first full-time employee in 2012. That person who's getting paid whether you're making money or not. Their family now depends on you. When I added her to the team, our production doubled. Her salary at the time was $28-$30,000 and we were making an additional $70,000. That absolutely makes sense from a business perspective.

And before we knew it, we were all at capacity so we brought on another full time employee and we doubled our production again. Again we hit capacity, so we brought on another person, and we doubled again. Once you hit a certain point, you stop doubling. You still grow but not double. For the first few years however, we doubled year over year.

As a result of that growth, in 2013, I decided to transform the team office into a full office. It felt like we had achieved a level of success that others may not see in a lifetime — all in a few short years.

In the past, I had been very secretive of the things I had been doing that led to our success. Now though, I thought, instead of keeping this a secret, why don't I help the others around me in our company be successful? Not one person can do it all, so why not make others successful? Around that time, I was also given the opportunity to buy the RE/MAX Concepts office in Ankeny, Iowa which would allow me to share my knowledge and help other agents with their success. In 2015, I opened another office in Ames. I also partner-owned three offices in what I consider the northern Des Moines metro territory. My motivation was that I wanted to help people be better versions of themselves.

When I started buying the additional offices, I decided to scale back on working with buyers. I had the Team agents do day to day things and I just managed the company, I worked with a very select few buyers and I focused primarily on listings, managing systems and people, and helping mentor.

By 2014, I had also let go of listings. I went on very few listing appointments. If I did have meetings to do with listings, they were select listings and they were also developer-builder type meetings. My focus was (and still is) more around managing systems day to day.

Our market share and our production was growing. In 2013 and 2014 we stayed about the same in production which was around $24 million. Then in 2015 it jumped to $32 million. In 2016, it was over $40 million. I wasn't even a full-fledged owner in Real Estate Concepts at that point, just a partner in a few offices. Honestly, from a business perspective, I didn't really care what the production was, I was making decisions based on where I wanted to spend my time.

I know people in this business who make a million-plus a year. They make a lot of money. But they're in their fifties and sixties and they have no family. They have no kids. They have nothing but money. They're literally miserable and that's no way to live.

The agents who thrive in this business have certain characteristics that make them great at what they do. They're organized. They put their family first. Nothing gets in the way of that. They're involved. And by involved, I mean they're in other groups, other organizations. It could be a church or it could be anything else where they are part of a community.

But their biggest asset is that they're just calm. If a deal falls apart, it happens. They don't get worked up. It's just part of business. It's a common trait in almost all of them.

Getting into flips and home building

We had up to 15 investors doing flips or rentals that we worked with regularly.

One of my biggest investors asked me at one point, "Hey, would you have an interest in this?" And my first reaction was, "No." After a period of saying no, I started thinking, "Well, why not?" So, if there was a deal that they didn't want, I'd maybe look at it and if it made sense, I would do it. I didn't want to do it at large scale because I didn't want to compete with my clients.

I did two in one year and I skipped a year without doing any. Around the beginning of 2016, I had a situation where the builder that I was working with took a big hit during the housing crisis and they were a bit reserved, which I respect. We had some clients who wanted to build a house and so I went to a developer I knew and asked, "Hey, can I buy this lot?" and he said, "Well, no, but I have eight left. I'll sell you eight."

"I don't want eight. I only want one. How about I buy two?" and he came back with,

"How about eight?"

This went on for a few months and finally I bought all eight lots. Then the client that I originally bought them for backed out of the deal which left me stuck with eight lots, so now what do I do?

I told the developer what had just happened and he said something to me that really resonated. I said, "Now I'm stuck with eight lots. I never wanted to be back into this and now here I am." He said, "Yeah, but if you control the land, you control the building."

So my solution was to put up listings with proposed constructions. I started to generate custom home orders from the listings. The builder would then buy my lot from me and build the custom home orders. This went well for a while, so I decided to do a little bit more. I started financing the deals myself, meaning I would do the construction loans, the builder would build it and we'd split the profit. In addition, we'd make our real estate fee.

That went on for about a year and because some of those projects weren't as profitable as they could have been, I decided to take an on another initiative to control the expenses. I had a full staff, a marketing team, an in-house accountant — I had everything I needed to take the next step.

So, I started my own building company. I went to both of those other people and said, "Hey, this is what I'm gonna do. Do you guys wanna be a part of it?" One guy said "Yeah" – who is now the project manager. He runs both construction companies. So, I started a home building company and now it runs on its own. I have to answer questions every now and then, but the same guy that I worked for listing his homes for years runs my company.

Again, it was just opportunity. I was trying to figure out a way to get deals done.

We always carried a high listing inventory but we also helped create my own listing inventory. It's pretty cool when my team sells the buy-side and list-side of one of our construction properties.

Buying RE/MAX Concepts

In March 2016, I was attending a RE/MAX Conference in Arizona, with my current partners and the owner of our company at the time. We were standing around at a networking event when the owner, completely out of the blue, said "I want you four to buy me out." His initial proposal was for him to retain the servicing company, while we purchased the existing offices.

After months of research and negotiation, the four of us purchased both the existing offices and servicing company for RE/MAX Real Estate Concepts on November 1st, 2016.

Currently, RE/MAX Concepts agents are the #2 ranked real estate company in the state of Iowa and the largest RE/MAX in Nebraska and Iowa. Our focus, from the time we purchased the offices and servicing company, has been to help every agent grow and succeed to the best of their ability. I am very honored and proud to be a part of all they have accomplished.

It's strange how things come full circle...

Back in 2010, when I was doing odd construction jobs to make ends meet, the last job that I did for my friend who had the construction company, was putting the deck around a historic mansion in Des Moines on Grand Avenue. At the time, the people were getting ready to use it as a law firm.

In early 2017, one of my partners called and said, "Hey, we should try to buy this place." We were trying to move one of our offices downtown. As I looked it up, I realized the place he wanted to buy was the mansion I had worked on — the last deck project that I had done for my friend. It's probably one of the neatest things in regards to my story. Within essentially seven years, I went from bankruptcy to owning the mansion that I had worked on to make ends meet.

So much can happen in real estate in a short time IF you're committed to your own success!

PART THREE:
THE ROADMAP

While the road I took to get to $20M and beyond may look slightly different than yours, there are some fundamental directions I can provide you to help you achieve the level of success you're looking for. Part Three is The Roadmap and it consists of several steps for you to take to achieve the same, each of which you'll read about in the coming chapters.

The Roadmap that I lay out in this section isn't for everyone, because not everyone will share the exact same values, personalities, or work ethic. Perhaps selling $20M or more in real estate isn't a goal for you, but building a business that works FOR you, not BECAUSE of you is. You'll get an immense amount of value from the following pages.

CHAPTER SEVEN:

Determine Your Destination

Twenty million in real estate is not what I had set out to do.

I was going to do my best with these two things in mind — my family would come first in building this business, and I had nothing to lose (because I'd basically lost it already!).

For your own personal journey on the road to $20M, the first step is getting crystal clear on the vision for your business.

Create your vision

Creating your vision is taking the dreams that you have for your life, and for your career, and planning each detail out to be so crystal clear, it becomes the blueprint you leverage to determine your goals and build your reality.

Get specific on how you'll spend your time, what kind of clients you'll work with, where the business will come from, how you'll grow and learn through the process, and ultimately, what the numbers are that you're looking to hit from a sales and income perspective.

Put these numbers around you everywhere so you see them throughout the day. Get your family, friends, and co-workers on the same page as you so they become your accountability partners.

I cannot state firmly enough how important a dialed in vision of your business is. The more clear the vision, the more likely it will happen.

Know your why

I encourage you to know your "why." Why do you want a business like this? What does it/will it give you? Why are you in real estate in the first place? Why do you get up every morning excited to do more of this work?

For those that know their why, the days become that much easier when prospects aren't returning calls, agents aren't answering emails, or deals bomb at the last minute because of the lender.

What are your values?

In addition to your vision and your why, determine what your values are. Especially those that you'll forever be committed to in your business.

I'm often asked how I achieved balance between work and family and the answer is simple. Family is one of my highest values. Take a look at my calendar and you'll see the times marked off for family take a higher priority than any last minute client request.

The goals that you're setting need to be aligned with your values. In fact, they should support them. So if exercise or health is a high priority for you, you'll have to align your priorities to achieve the goal of being healthy. Particularly in a business like this that can occupy ALL of your time if you let it.

You can build a business in real estate that serves your life if you remember the following elements of the first Roadmap:

1. **Know your why.** This business can be both challenging and rewarding. By knowing *why* you are in real estate, you'll be able to weather all of

the emotional, financial and time challenges along the way without second guessing your decision to get in this business in the first place.

2. **Define your core values.** What 4 or 5 values will you commit to living your life and business with? Once you know what these are, your business decisions become far easier. As an example, if security is one of your core values, you may not take the risks that I took in my business and instead opt for more "sure thing" investments.

3. **Establish your vision for success.** Your vision *will* change over time. When I started in real estate, my focus was to save my family's home and get out of the mess I was in. I hit $20 Million in production in less than four years. We've since blown past that number as a team and the vision has grown with my growing team and businesses. Yours will too, and to get there you must establish a crystal clear vision for what success looks like NOW. Post it everywhere as a reminder of what you're working for.

CHAPTER EIGHT:

Plan For Passengers

This chapter is probably one of the most important of all in the Road To $20 Million.

This is simply because while you may be the only one in your family that's *in* real estate, your entire family is actually in real estate with you. This business has a tendency to take over family schedules, change the dynamic between husbands and wives, and can become like a needy child if you don't set it up right.

The next roadmap is to *Plan For Passengers*.

The "passengers" I refer to could be spouses, family, partners in business, mentors and others in your network. Whether you're new to the business or you've been selling homes for awhile, this roadmap is an essential piece of getting to $20M.

The main objective is to consider the people you're surrounding yourself with on your journey and talking about (and setting) expectations ahead of time.

Your support structure in real estate begins at home.

Your spouse or significant other has as much a role to play in your success as anyone on your real estate team. One of the most important things my wife and I did was set the expectations about when I'd work and when I wouldn't.

Again, knowing that family is one of my core values, if I'm committed to making all of my kids' events, I can easily tell clients "I have an appointment" and stay true to that value.

What I see more than anything in real estate is sacrificing family or spouses for the business. It's a surefire way to have a significant other that begins to resent what you do for a living. After all, it may start to feel like you're trading one for the other.

Inside The Road To $20 Million Course we go into detail about how to create The Spouse Agreement which includes the critical questions you both must ask each other. The Spouse Agreement will help you align your priorities to maintain a positive balance at home and at work, as well as a support structure on the road ahead.

To get started though, simply having the conversation with your spouse is a great place to start. Define when you'll work and when you won't and communicate this to your spouse.

It's just as critical to have on-going expectation conversations with your partners, team members, lenders, inspectors, and support staff. Ultimately, real estate is a team sport. Nothing closes without first being touched by a number of people. So, clarifying expectations up front with the people you work with helps make sure you won't be blindsided by issues later.

As an example, I encourage real estate agents to communicate expectations to lenders that if anything appears to be holding up a transaction to keep them (the real estate agent) updated. Every agent has been burned at one point or another with a deal bombing at the last minute for reasons that could've been addressed up front.

In Part Two I wrote about how I leveraged relationships and my network to build the business.

As you *Plan For Passengers*, give some thought to the people that will support you along the way. If you're new to a community or don't want to rely on those close to you, what will you do to build your name in the areas you're focused on? Getting involved in groups/organizations outside of real estate will help you create a name for yourself without "in your face" marketing.

As I mentioned, just being on a committee or being a member of the Chamber of Commerce isn't enough. You must become involved in these activities with an understanding that you'll be rewarded with referrals and business in time. My involvement in the Chamber of Commerce has done wonders for my business and given me an incredible network of people to lean on.

CHAPTER NINE:

Find Your Fuel & Efficiency

One of the biggest obstacles that I've seen in real estate agents is their ability to create efficiencies in their business. And as a result of the inefficiencies that are occurring regularly, they aren't able to produce what they're truly capable of. You might say they can't get out of their own way long enough to find true success.

From the day I started in real estate, my time was always something that I paid close attention to and you should too. After all, there will always be more money, but no one is making more time. The only thing that can ever happen with time is spending it, and it's up to you to determine how best to spend your time.

The goal of this chapter is to help you maintain your motivation in the business through focusing your energy on creating systems. When the systems in your business are working flawlessly, the systems actually run the business. No matter who you plug into an excellent system, you should be getting excellent results.

One such system is how you calendar your appointments and other obligations. In our offices, we use Google Calendar exclusively and we all have visibility with each other's calendars.

You can get really creative about how you color code listing or sales appointments, family events, and networking meetings. But the most important part of using the calendar, in my opinion, is blocking your time out to knock out certain tasks.

Nothing happens unless it's in the calendar, so my team, my spouse, and my partners all know that this system is what keeps me most efficient and the expectation is they'll use it accordingly.

Some of the systems I created at the beginning of my business are still running efficiently. We've tweaked and modified them over time as technology changed, but the end result is still the same — we get leads, listings and sales!

One of the first lessons I learned in marketing myself was consistency matters. So, I built a system to send postcard mailers to a particular zip code and I have team members that execute that system every month.

Once a system is in place and we know that it produces results, we simply make sure it happens. We modify it every now and again, test the results, and keep moving forward. Efficiently.

If you're lucky enough to have a team working with you, make sure that you're being incredibly intentional with the team as much as possible. At first, I was skeptical about bringing other people into the business with me, but then I realized that if I have 40 hours to work a week (more like 50-60 realistically) having another person on my team gives me another 40 hours. Now I've got 80 hours of productivity to leverage. In the RT20M course, I go into greater detail about how my team and I create efficiencies, leverage systems, and hold each other accountable to them.

When You Do What You Do

Staying healthy is one of my core values, and I found that attempting to squeeze workouts in late in the day or the afternoon just didn't work. I'm a guy that has a lot to do, so to maintain my health and stay efficient with my time, I get up early to hit the gym. This isn't ideal for everyone, but if you're going to maximize your time, you've got to decide what are the most important things to accomplish as well as decide when you're going to tackle them (while focused on your goals).

This applies to networking functions, client lunches, kids' events, putting up signs, posting listings, running errands, etc. The blessing and curse of real estate is you have relative flexibility of your time. Oftentimes, this means that agents spin their wheels doing non-productive activities when they could be super productive and efficient.

If you know that you run low on energy right after lunch, perhaps doing errands or putting out signs or networking meetings are best suited for these hours.

If you know that you're a night owl, how can you best leverage your energy at night to maintain productivity?

Finally, what is the fuel of your day? This may seem like an obvious statement, but if you're putting junk in your body, you'll probably feel like junk throughout the day.

You have the ability to make *significant* money in real estate, but it's going to require you to be at your best as much as possible.

Here's why — you'll have moments where everything in your world is challenged. And the one thing that will determine whether or not you achieve your vision is how much grit you have to get through it. Grit is the one thing that has kept me on the Road To $20 Million and beyond. It's the one trait that I can't teach other people to have. You either have it or you have to foster it.

In this step of the Road to $20 Million, I break down how to add fuel to your business and how to create efficiencies through systems creation and leveraging the skills of your team.

Remember the following three things as you take this journey:

1. On a daily basis, maintain your motivation and focus to achieve your goals.
2. Maximize your time and your energy.
3. Implement systems in your business and life to create efficiencies.

CHAPTER TEN

Engage In The Journey

To be a professional real estate agent, you must do business, not just play business.

What that means to me is you must engage in the journey of building a $20M real estate business, even if you're in your first month. This business is wonderful for those who are playing the long game. After all, if clients buy from you and they're happy with the service you provided, then logic would tell you that they'll come back and use you again. Especially if you've built in all of the systems mentioned here—in the book and in greater detail inside the course—that help you foster and keep the relationship top of mind.

As a team, we spend lots of time evaluating the steps of the sales process and how to build an incredible relationship with our clients. We talk through how to adjust to changing market conditions and demographics to build our list. And we are working all the time to turn names (or leads) on our list into qualified buyers and sellers.

Being a real estate agent is so much more than just helping people buy and sell homes. It's as much about being an incredible marketer, a social media strategist, a professional networker, a systems-minded entrepreneur, and a leader in your community.

The Road To $20 Million requires that you engage in the journey of becoming the agent that can produce, build a team, weather the tough times, and ultimately create a lasting business that begins to work harder than you do. That may mean engaging others around you that excel in areas that you don't.

There's an old African proverb that says: "If you want to go fast, go alone, but if you want to go far, go together."

The three easiest ways to get *Engaged In The Journey* are:

1. **Build your database.** Right from day one you should be focused on building a massive list of people who are familiar with you. These people

will be the sources of ongoing sales and listings well into the future.

2. **Know your market.** Your knowledge of the market will help in listing appointments, in selling various areas, and in answering questions from a place of credibility. Spend time learning the ins and outs of your market and become the go-to expert.

3. **Convert leads to clients.** Think about how you might convert those who merely know of you to those who refer you, sell through you, or buy through you. It's about building a relationship with people over time by providing great content, value, and expertise whether you've met them or not.

CHAPTER ELEVEN:

Explore Your Options (for Business Entrepreneurs)

One of the things I realized early on in my real estate career was all of the different ways you could generate revenue as an agent. When no one else was interested in doing BPOs, I made $50,000 in one year doing them. That willingness to test a different model of making money as an agent led me to learn everything I could about short sales, thereby become a top performing agent on the side of town that had a ton of BPOs and short sales.

The same thing happened when I ventured into doing flips, building homes, opening my own office, hiring agents, and buying out the broker with my partners.

While you're on The Road To $20 Million, keep your eyes open to other potential sources of revenue. The RT20M Course goes into greater depth and detail of the various ways to build diversified sources of business income, but for now keep this in mind — the market will trend one way or another and those who figure out how to stabilize their income no matter how the market is trending will always be on top.

I think it's important to know your business, be able to identify opportunities, and to always be learning. A lot of people want success, but only as it fits in their checklist — right location, right time, right amount of effort, etc. You have to look outside the box and if something doesn't work, you figure out how it could, while remembering to stay true to who you are. Keep an open mind and remain flexible to allow for growth and adjustments to your vision and goals. Don't hold so tight to your success criteria that you prevent success from happening all together.

CHAPTER TWELVE:

Drive Your Brand and Your Business

Whether you know it or not, you are creating your brand on a daily basis. Everything from the marketing you use, the way you dress, even the way you drive could be impacting your business either positively or negatively.

Marketing will be the lifeblood of your business and having a well thought out and executed plan will make all the difference to get you on the road. In this chapter, you'll learn about brand awareness and promoting your business.

Brand Awareness

So, the primary objective at the beginning of your business should be to identify what your brand is. Will you build your reputation specializing in listings only?

Are you an agent that's going to only work on listings above a certain amount? When people see your signage, what do you want them to think or say? When you're out in public, how will you present yourself to stay consistent with your branding?

A few examples of Realtors who have done this:

1) Realtor A specializes in the Luxury Market because it is who he is — he has the cars, the house, the clothes, the image. It's not a show, it's his lifestyle.

2) Realtor B is referral based — she spends very little money on marketing. She is great at building relationships and staying in contact with her referrals.

3) Realtor C specializes in new construction, represents many builders and is all in and focuses primarily in one community. This Realtor works, lives and plays in this community.

A common denominator in all three of these Realtors is they are giving not only their money but their time — they give back to their community and those around them.

Building a marketing strategy and specific content around that is key to creating a very specific brand in your area.

When I started promoting myself I had very little money and went for the most cost-effective approach I could — direct mail postcards. To this day the postcards still go out on a regular basis and are just as consistent in messaging today as they were the first day they were sent.

As I began to see success with the postcards, I bought advertising on a bus bench in the area where a majority of my short sales were coming from. That bus bench has generated tens of thousands of dollars in commissions over the past several years and continues to produce today.

Promotion

As my listings and sales client base grew, so did my systems around marketing to that list. We send an average of 10,0000 emails a month to a list that continues to grow week by week. The people who have bought and sold with me are one of the greatest sources of business I could ask for because they know what to expect with me: consistency.

They hear from me so regularly, they've just grown to expect it.

The content that we send out to our clients is a variety of things. I was one of the very first customers of a service called Referral Squirrel (*https://www.thereferralsquirrel.com/*). The service arranges discounts of all kinds (restaurants, sporting event tickets, activities, etc.) and then does direct mail pieces to the list we provide. In our emails, we include recipes, scheduled events in the community, and facts about the real estate market.

Your goal should be to include things of value so there is a reason for your prospects and clients to open the email or read the direct mail piece.

The key to driving your brand and your business is to take a very long-term perspective.

The typical family lives in a home no more than four years, so if you can set up your systems in the first 2-4 years effectively, the rest of your career should be a breeze. The repeat business you'll receive from treating your clients right, coupled with the referrals you get from them will have you on the Road To $20 Million in no time.

CHAPTER THIRTEEN

Enjoy The Ride and See The Sights

There are two thoughts I want to leave you with as you find yourself on the road with me. Both of these concepts have made an incredible difference in my life both personally and professionally.

The first is keeping your eyes open to opportunities to create passive income.

Being in real estate has a distinct advantage because we get to see properties coming on the market before anyone else does. The "deals" that can be found are numerous if you're looking for them and prepared to act on them when they appear.

Investing in real estate has created a passive income stream for me and my family that allows us to sleep peacefully at night, no matter what is happening in the business.

Real estate can be a very up and down business depending on the local and national economy. In the major metro area where we operate, there are two major employers that hire tens of thousands of people. When they start talking about layoffs, the market can shift in a hurry.

Having some forms of passive income can create stability in your business that will allow you to take risks that others won't be able to take. As shared in Part Two, I took a fair number of those risks that paid off enormously.

Consider putting aside a certain percentage of each check for the purpose of investing in passive income properties. How and what you invest in is up to you, but I cover passive income sources and how to identify those opportunities in the RT20M course. The beauty of passive income is doing the work once and getting paid over and over and over and over again.

The second thought I'd like to leave you with is the importance of giving back.

The gifts that we're given are meant to be shared and nothing has been so rewarding for me and my family as being able to give back to causes and charities we believe in.

Whether it's your church, local food pantries, national charities, or even the school district near you, think about the ways that you could be giving back as your business grows... I feel it is our duty as business owners to do so.

I hope you have enjoyed this book and look forward to seeing you on the Road to $20 Million.

NEXT STEPS

If the information covered here has you left you wanting more, the Road To $20M Course is a deep dive into each of the chapters covered in this book. The course will guide you through each of the steps you'll be taking along the way, shared by me, with support to help you while you're "on the road."

My team has also created downloadable worksheets that will help you through each step. You'll find the download links in each chapter and I encourage you to download those pdf documents and follow along accordingly. My real estate career has been loaded with twists and turns, but my mindset has always been you either win or you learn!

As a result of that philosophy, I've been able to build a highly productive team, bought out my broker (and now help manage over 100 agents), flipped dozens of properties, and live a life that I once thought was extremely out of reach.

Your real estate career may be speeding along or you may be stuck in traffic. No matter the case, my goal is to help you get on the Road To $20 Million. That means different things for different people — for some it might mean selling another 50 sides this year, for others it might mean building a team and expanding your marketing reach, and still others might be interested in property or land development.

I'm here to help you go anywhere you want to go.

So, let's get started with the roadmap that got me where I am today. Go here http://roadto20million.com/RT2Mbookgift to download the Mindset and Goal Setting Roadmap **at no cost to you** to get you laser focused on your goals AND how you're going to get yourself there.

Being on this journey with me will take dedication, discipline, and drive — along the way I'll encourage you, share resources with you, and answer questions you may have.

ABOUT THE AUTHOR

Shane Torres is a partner-owner for one of the top ranked real estate brokerages in the nation, RE/MAX Concepts.

He is the owner of one of the top producing real estate teams at both the state and national level, and is an entrepreneur/owner of several additional business ventures with multi-million dollar revenues.

He is a valued coach, consultant and presenter.

Shane has a lifetime of experience in overcoming adversity and more than 20 years experience in the housing industry.

He is passionate about sharing his experience with others to inspire professional and personal growth in line with their personal values.

Faith, family, and giving back are important to Shane and are the values he contributes as the foundation to his success. Married with three children, he lives in Polk City, IA.

You can connect with Shane here:
www.roadto20million.com

Can you help?

Loved the book? On your way to $20M?!

If you enjoyed the book, I'd love it if you left your honest review on the site you purchased this book from.

This will help more people find this book and allow me to update the next version with your feedback.

Thanks so much for your support, it means a lot.

Shane Torres

Made in USA - Kendallville, IN
30417_9780578497815
03.14.2022 0931